# LEOPARD TORTOISE CARE AND OWNERSHIP

Everything You Need To Know About Leopard Tortoise Breeding, Feeding And Nutrition, Habitat, Housing, Conversation, Health Care, Common Diseases And Why They Make Great Pets.

**BY**

**RAPH FRANCIS**

# <u>*TABLE OF CONTENTS*</u>

<u>*CHAPTER 1:*</u>

# INTRODUCING LEOPARD TORTOISES

Stigmochelys pardalis, or leopard tortoises, are among the most common kinds of tortoises kept as pets because of their eye-catching appearance, small stature, and typically calm disposition. They are visually striking because of their exquisitely patterned shells, which are speckled with black and yellow dots like a leopard's coat. These tortoises, which are native to the savannas of eastern and southern Africa, need a long-term commitment from any potential owner since they may live for many decades. This chapter will discuss their history, the reasons they make desirable pets, and the things prospective owners should know before bringing one into their home.

## *Background and Native Environment*

Native to semi-arid areas of eastern and southern Africa, including Sudan, Ethiopia, and South Africa, are leopard tortoises. They are found in grasslands, scrublands, and savannas, where they eat mostly succulent plants, shrubs, and grasses. Pet owners who want to reproduce the perfect environment for their pet in captivity should take into account the fact that their natural habitat is characterized by a diversity of temperatures and environmental conditions.

Leopard tortoises are mostly solitary animals in the wild, where they spend most of their days grazing and warming themselves in the sun. Leopard tortoises do not hibernate, in contrast to several other species, however they could become less active in the winter. One of the reasons they are well-liked by pet owners is because of their kind disposition and reasonably submissive nature.

## *The Physical Properties*

Adult leopard tortoises may grow to be medium to large-sized animals, measuring between 10 to 18 inches in length, while some are capable of becoming much bigger. They get their name from their high-domed shells, or carapaces, which are decorated with unique black and yellow patterns that resemble a leopard's spots. The degree and form of these patterns may differ across people; some may have more subdued marks, while others may exhibit a more striking contrast. Their unique shell protects them from natural predators in addition to enhancing their visual appeal.

Leopard tortoises have strong, robust legs that are designed for them to move great distances in their native environment in pursuit of food. They can efficiently feed on grasses and plants because of their powerful beaks, and many potential predators are repelled by their comparatively enormous size. The gentle nature of Leopard tortoises, in spite of their size, makes them popular among those who like tortoises.

### *Reasons for Choosing a Pet Leopard Tortoise?*

There are several reasons why people choose to keep leopard tortoises as pets. First off, if their basic requirements are satisfied, they are not as difficult to care for as some other kinds of tortoises. They don't need a very specific diet since they are herbivores and follow an easy diet. They are also gentle and calm creatures, which makes them ideal for those looking for a low-maintenance, non-aggressive pet.

They are a beautiful addition to any reptile collection due to their stunning look and elaborately patterned shell. Although they have the potential to grow to large sizes, most keepers who have enough room can still handle them. Their durability is another alluring feature. If given the correct care, leopard tortoises may live for 50 to 100 years in captivity, making them a dependable companion for their owners. But with such a long life span also comes the need to make sure the tortoise receives proper care for the whole of its existence.

Leopard tortoises are a fantastic blend of beauty, hardiness, and simplicity of maintenance for those who have a like for reptiles in general and tortoises in particular. They may even get somewhat accustomed to their owners and are not hostile. It's crucial to remember that these tortoises need particular care and a long-term commitment in order to flourish.

## *CHAPTER 2:*

# COMPREHENDING THE BEHAVIOR OF LEOPARD TORTOISES

Due to their reputation for being placid and gentle, leopard tortoises are a popular option among pet owners looking for a low-maintenance, quiet reptile. But in order to provide them the greatest care possible, you must comprehend their behavior. Their general temperament, grazing habits, and interactions with people are all important aspects of their behavior patterns that determine how well they do in captivity. To assist owners better appreciate their special qualities, we shall examine the several facets of Leopard tortoise behavior in this chapter.

### *Typical Attributes and Behaviors*

Leopard tortoises are generally solitary animals, both in the wild and in captivity. Being herbivores, they graze for a large portion of the day on a range of grasses, weeds, and leafy greens. Their desire to seek for food and bask in order to regulate their body temperature is what essentially drives their activity. Like other tortoise species, leopard tortoises are renowned for their methodical and very sluggish movements.

Leopard tortoises are migratory grazers in their native environment, which means they graze across large regions in search of food. They exhibit a similar habit when kept in captivity, when they need enough room to roam about and feed. It's crucial to make sure their container is safe even though they aren't known to climb or dig deeply. Instead, they could try to investigate it by strolling around its perimeter.

The way leopard tortoises react to varying weather conditions is an intriguing feature of their nature. They are used to a range of temperatures in their natural savannas, from hot days to chilly nights. They have therefore evolved to control their body temperature by hiding or finding shade during the hotter parts of the day and basking in the sun during the colder months. If you want to replicate their natural behavior in captivity, you must provide them access to both cooler shaded regions and locations for basking.

## Communication with People

In general, leopard tortoises are peaceful and do not attack people. They may approach when food is presented in response to regular feeding schedules since they are able to identify their owners. It is crucial to remember that leopard tortoises do not develop the same social ties with people as mammals do, just like all other reptiles. Since they are not social beings, they may survive without interacting with people or other tortoises.

Nevertheless, with careful treatment, leopard tortoises may get used to being handled gently, and some may even put up with being stroked or lifted up. Handling should be limited, however, since tortoises like to investigate their environment on their own. It's crucial to provide a Leopard tortoise with stable body support while lifting it to prevent strain or damage. Refrain from shaking or turning the turtle over on its head since these actions may injure or confuse it.

Additionally well-known for being rather quiet pets are leopard tortoises. Other than the odd hiss or grunt in response to being frightened or while mating, they do not produce much noise. They convey themselves mostly via body language and nonverbal communication. For instance, a Leopard tortoise may stretch its head and limbs when it is at ease and calm, or it may withdraw within its shell if it senses danger.

*Safe Ways to Care for Your Tortoise*

Leopard tortoises need to be handled carefully to prevent stress or harm. Because they are not used to being picked up or carried, unlike dogs or cats, tortoises may become nervous or hostile when handled incorrectly. Here are some pointers for caring for your Leopard tortoise:

*1. Approach Slowly:* Always take a calm, measured approach to your turtle. They could get frightened by sudden movements and hide within their shells.

*2. hold Their Body:* Use both hands to hold the body of a Leopard tortoise as you are taking it up. To stabilize it, place one hand beneath its shell and the other on its back. Holding them by their tails or limbs might hurt them, so stay away from it.

***3. Keep Handling Minimal:*** Although leopard tortoises can withstand little handling, it's crucial to avoid giving them too much attention. Being solitary beings, they would rather be allowed to investigate their environment.

***4. Avoid Stressful Situations:*** Handling tortoises harshly or placing them in strange or unpleasant places might cause stress in them. To reduce tension, always deal with them in a composed, controlled manner.

Pet owners may foster an atmosphere that enhances their tortoise's pleasure and well-being by learning about the behavior of leopard tortoises. Acknowledging these lovely animals' need for space, appropriate temperature control, and careful care can help to ensure them long and healthy lives.

## *CHAPTER 3:*

# ESTABLISHING THE IDEAL ENVIRONMENT

For the sake of a leopard tortoise's health and welfare, the perfect environment must be created. Given that these tortoises are indigenous to semi-arid parts of Africa, it is imperative that their captive habitat closely resembles their natural surroundings. Despite their reputation for durability, leopard tortoises cannot survive in every environment. For them to live comfortably, certain requirements for substrate, lighting, temperature, and space must be met.

Whether your Leopard tortoise is inside or outdoors, this chapter offers comprehensive setup instructions that will help it feel right at home.

## Interior versus External Enclosures

Choosing whether to keep your Leopard tortoise inside, outdoors, or a mix of both is one of the first choices you will need to make while putting up a habitat. Every choice has pros and cons, and your geographic location, climate, and amount of accessible space will all play a major role in your selection.

### Outside Covers:

The ideal enclosures for leopard tortoises are outdoors, particularly if you reside in a warm environment. They may enjoy the natural sunshine outside, which contains UVB rays that are vital to their health. These enclosures need to be roomy, safe, and as closely modeled like the tortoise's native habitat as feasible.

- *Space:* Outdoor cages must have adequate room for the tortoises to move about and feed. Given that mature leopard tortoises may reach lengths of up to 18 inches, it is advised that they be kept in a spacious habitat of at least 100 square feet. There should be wide spaces for sunbathing and shady locations for cooling down inside the cage.

- *Fencing:* To keep your tortoise from straying, you must install a sturdy fence or barrier. To stop digging, the walls should be dug a few inches into the earth and at least 12 to 18 inches high. Although they are not known to dig deep burrows, leopard tortoises may try to get out if they see an opening.

*- Shelter:* It's critical to provide a hiding place or shelter. This might be a little hut or a home for tortoises where they can hide from bad weather. The shelter has to be insulated in colder areas to shield the tortoise from the chilly nighttime temperatures.

*- Plants and Grazing Area:* Since leopard tortoises are grazers, providing their enclosure with edible plants like dandelions and grasses helps promote their natural foraging habits. Verify that the enclosure's flora are suitable for tortoises to consume and not harmful.

*Interior Sheds:*

If you live in a cooler location or during the winter, when the outdoors are unfavorable for Leopard tortoises, you may need to install inside cages. A huge tortoise's enclosure must be properly built, since maintaining one inside might be difficult.

- *Size:* The enclosure must be large enough for the tortoise to go about, even if there is less room inside. For an adult, an enclosure should be at least 6 feet by 6 feet, but the bigger the better.

- *Temperature Control:* You must establish a temperature gradient within the cage since interior spaces lack natural heat. The ideal temperature range for leopard tortoises is 75°F to 90°F, with a basking area of around 95°F.

Under-tank heaters and heating lights may assist in preserving these conditions.

*- illumination:* In order for Leopard tortoises to manufacture vitamin D3, which aids in their calcium metabolism and maintenance of strong bones, UVB illumination is necessary. Insufficient UVB exposure may lead to metabolic bone disease in tortoises. To ensure continued efficacy, full-spectrum UVB bulbs should be positioned no more than 12 inches from the basking area and replaced every six months.

*- Substrate:* For indoor enclosures, selecting the appropriate substrate is crucial. To mimic their native environment, a blend of sand, coconut fiber, and organic soil works nicely. Substrates

such as pine or cedar shavings should be avoided since they might be toxic if consumed.

### *Requirements for Temperature, Lighting, and Humidity*

Maintaining the proper environmental conditions in your Leopard tortoise's indoor and outdoor habitats is essential to its health. Since they are ectothermic, or cold-blooded, creatures, their body temperature is controlled by outside heat sources.

### *Climate:*

In their native environment, Leopard tortoises have warm days and cold nights. The cage must include a temperature gradient in order to allow the tortoise to wander between warmer and colder regions as required in order to simulate this. The ideal daytime temperature is to stay between 75°F and 85°F, with a basking region that may go as high as 95°F. Temperatures may dip to around 70°F at night, but they shouldn't go below 65°F since it would stress the tortoise and cause health problems.

*- Basking Spot:* To help the tortoise warm up in the mornings or after meals, a special basking place should be prepared with a ceramic heater or heat lamp. This point should be situated at one end of the cage to create a gradient.

### Lighting

The optimum source of UVB is natural sunshine, however UVB bulbs are necessary inside. For general health and the absorption of calcium, UVB exposure is essential. The recommended duration of the light should be 10 to 12 hours each day to replicate the cycle of natural sunshine.

**- *UVB Bulbs:*** Put a full-spectrum UVB bulb meant for reptiles in the basking section. Even if it seems to be functioning, change the bulb every six months since its UVB output decreases with time.

### Humidity:

The ideal humidity range for leopard tortoises is between 40% and 60%. Even though they come from semi-arid regions, they nonetheless need some humidity to avoid dehydration and problems with their shells. You may assist maintain the right humidity levels by offering a small water dish and misting the cage. But take care not to over humidify the enclosure—too much moisture might cause respiratory illnesses.

## *Design of Substrate and Enclosure*

For leopard tortoises, the selection of substrate is essential since it affects their capacity to burrow, keep hydrated, and maintain hygiene. The ideal substrate should resemble the grasses and dirt that are present in their natural habitat.

- *Soil-Sand Mixture:* Organic topsoil mixed with sand is a good mixture for Leopard tortoises. It helps control the moisture level in the cage and allows them to dig a little. Make sure the sand isn't too fine since breathing in it might lead to respiratory problems.

- *Grass or Hay:* In outdoor situations, some owners choose to border the enclosure with hay or grass. This gives the tortoise a gentle surface to graze and stroll on.

- *Avoid Harmful Substrates:* Cedar and pine shavings should be avoided, since they contain fragrant oils that might irritate a tortoise's respiratory system. Furthermore, if consumed, substrates like gravel or tiny stones may be harmful.

- *Water Dish:* The tortoise should always have access to a shallow water dish for drinking. It should be big enough for the tortoise to soak if desired, but shallow enough to avoid drowning.

- *Hide Areas:* Your tortoise's mental health depends on having hiding places in the enclosure. Logs, stones, or commercial reptile skins may be used to make them. When a tortoise feels threatened or needs to relax, its hides provide them with a feeling of security and a place to hide.

In conclusion, careful consideration of a Leopard tortoise's natural activities, environmental requirements, and size is necessary while building up the ideal home. For their long-term health and enjoyment, whether housed inside or outdoors, the proper temperature, lighting, substrate, and space must be provided. Taking care of a tortoise is a very satisfying experience, especially when you can bring out its natural behaviors in addition to ensuring its survival with a well-designed cage.

## *<u>CHAPTER 4:</u>*

# LEOPARD TORTOISE NUTRITION AND DIET

The general health and lifespan of leopard tortoises are greatly influenced by their food and nutrition. These tortoises need a carefully balanced diet that resembles what they would eat in the wild since they are herbivores. Giving children an unhealthy or imbalanced diet may cause major health problems including obesity, intestinal disorders, and metabolic bone disease. In this chapter, we will discuss the key components of a Leopard tortoise's diet, including the sorts of foods they should consume, the significance of calcium and vitamins, and items to avoid to preserve maximum health.

## Optimal Foods and Feeding Plans

Since leopard tortoises are mostly grazers, they spend the majority of their time searching for food in the environment, such as grasses, leaves, and other plant materials. It is important to support this instinctive grazing habit in captivity by feeding them a diet high in low-protein, high-fiber plant materials.

### Weeds and Grasses:

A Leopard tortoise's food should mostly consist of different types of grasses and weeds. These provide the tortoise's digestive tract the essential fiber it needs to help with digestion and maintain optimal health. The following are some of the finest weeds and grasses for leopard tortoises:

***Timothy Grass:*** Low in protein and high in fiber, Timothy grass is a great staple for feeding leopard tortoises.

- ***Bermuda Grass:*** This is an additional excellent grass substitute that grows well in outside enclosures.

- ***Dandelion Greens:*** Rich in vitamins and fiber, dandelions are a healthy and nutrient-dense vegetable.

- ***Clover:*** Another excellent source of fiber, clover is often favored by tortoises.

- ***Alfalfa:*** Although alfalfa is a nutritious crop, it should be given in moderation since it has greater protein and calcium content than other grasses.

***Vegetables:***

Apart from grasses, leopard tortoises may also be given a range of veggies to add to their diet. A fantastic option are leafy greens, which provide extra minerals including calcium and vitamins A and C. Vegetables that are suitable include:

- ***Collard Greens:*** A Leopard tortoise's diet would benefit greatly from the calcium-rich collard greens.

- ***Mustard Greens:*** Another green high in calcium, mustard greens should be eaten in moderation since they contain a small amount of oxalates, which have the ability to bind calcium.

- ***Kale:*** Rich in nutrients, kale should be eaten in moderation because of oxalates, much as mustard greens.

- ***Squash:*** To add some diversity to their diet, yellow squash and zucchini are excellent vegetable choices.

- ***Cactus Pads (Prickly Pear):*** Many Leopard tortoises like to eat cactus pads since they are an excellent source of nutrients and water.

***Fruits:***

Fruit should only be given to leopard tortoises in moderation and seldom as their digestive tracts are not designed to process the high sugar content of most fruits. Digestion problems such as diarrhea might result from consuming too much fruit. If you do serve fruit, limit it to bite-sized pieces of the following:

- Papaya
- Figs
- Melons
- Berries

It's crucial to remember that fruit should only account for 10% of their whole diet.

***Retail Tortoise Meals:***

A Leopard tortoise's diet should mostly consist of fresh grasses, vegetables, and sometimes fruits, although it is also possible to utilize commercial tortoise diets as a supplement. Make sure the commercial tortoise food you choose is made especially for grassland tortoises and has a high fiber content and a low protein content.

When fresh food is not accessible, these items might be helpful as nutritional supplements to provide a well-balanced diet.

## Calcium and Vitamin Importance

For leopard tortoises, calcium is one of the most important minerals since it supports the development of strong bones and a healthy shell. Serious health issues, such as metabolic bone disease, which is characterized by weak, malformed bones and a soft shell, may be brought on by an inadequate calcium intake. A diet rich in calcium is necessary to avoid this, as is appropriate UVB exposure for the creation of vitamin D3, which facilitates the absorption of calcium.

### Supplements with calcium:

It's often important to provide calcium supplements to make sure the tortoise is receiving adequate calcium, even with a well-balanced diet. A few times a week, the tortoise may get these supplements in the form of powdered calcium carbonate sprinkled over its meal.

***Calcium without Phosphorus:*** Verify that the calcium supplement you choose is free of phosphorus. Because too much phosphorus might obstruct the absorption of calcium, tortoises need a diet that is richer in calcium to phosphorus.

***Minerals and Vitamins:***
For optimum health, leopard tortoises need additional vitamins and minerals in addition to calcium, especially vitamins A and D. Although

a well-balanced diet may provide the majority of essential elements, vitamin supplements can be taken on occasion to avoid shortages. Supplementing with vitamins should be done so sparingly since taking too many of them might be hazardous.

***Vitamin D3:*** Mostly acquired via UVB sun exposure, this vitamin is necessary for the absorption of calcium. Vitamin D3 supplements may be necessary for tortoises housed inside who do not get enough UVB light, however it is best to use artificial or natural UV illumination instead.

### *Water and Hydration Requirements*

Like other tortoises, leopard tortoises need a steady supply of clean water. They come from semi-arid areas, yet they still need to drink enough water on a regular basis to be healthy. In addition to drinking water, Leopard tortoises will frequently soak in shallow water to hydrate and aid with digesting.

*- Water Dish:* Make sure there's always a big enough shallow water dish available for the tortoise to soak in and drink from. The dish should be big enough to enable the tortoise to enter comfortably but shallow enough to avoid drowning. To keep the water clean, it should be changed every day.

*Soaking:* Once or twice a week, particularly in hot weather or if your Leopard tortoise seems dehydrated, it's a good idea to immerse them in shallow water for 15 to 20 minutes. Soaking promotes healthy digestion and keeps their skin and shell moisturized.

**Foods You Should Avoid**

Although a large range of plant-based diets are suitable for leopard tortoises, some should be avoided because of possible toxicity or detrimental effects on the tortoise's health. Items to stay away from include:

*Spinach:* The high oxalates in spinach may bind to calcium and inhibit its absorption. Overfeeding spinach has been linked to the development of metabolic bone disease and calcium deficits.

- *Rhubarb:* Never feed rhubarb to tortoises due to its severe toxicity.

*- Iceberg Lettuce:* Mostly composed of water, iceberg lettuce has little nutritional value while not being harmful. It is not something that a Leopard tortoise should eat on a daily basis.

*- Animal Protein:* Since leopard tortoises are strict herbivores, they should never be given animal products like dairy, meat, or eggs. Feeding animal protein might cause health complications such as kidney stones.

*- Grains and Processed Foods:* Because they are not good for a tortoise's digestive system, do not give grains, bread, or any other processed human food.

In conclusion, your Leopard tortoise's long-term health and wellbeing depend on you feeding them a correct food and nutrition plan. They will acquire the nutrients they need to flourish if they eat a diet that resembles their natural grazing activity, which is mostly composed of high-fiber grasses and vegetables with sporadic fruits and supplements. You may contribute to your Leopard tortoise's long and healthy life by monitoring their calcium intake, giving them enough water, and keeping them away from unhealthful foods.

## *CHAPTER 5:*

# LEOPARD TORTOISE HABITAT AND ENCLOSURE SETUP

For a Leopard tortoise to have a healthy and long life, it has to have a suitable enclosure and environment. Regardless of whether it is housed inside or outside, the habitat has to closely resemble the natural environment in terms of substrate, space, temperature, humidity, lighting, and safety. Natural activities like digging, sunbathing, and grazing are encouraged in a well-designed enclosure and are beneficial to the physical and mental well-being of the tortoise. In this chapter, we will discuss the key aspects for making the ideal Leopard tortoise habitat.

### Interior Sheds

An indoor enclosure may provide a suitable habitat for those who live in areas with harsh weather or who want to keep their Leopard tortoises inside. However, careful design and upkeep are necessary to ensure the tortoise flourishes in this setting.

***Size of the Enclosure:*** Leopard tortoises are energetic creatures that require lots of area to wander, even inside. A little space will prevent them from exercising and may cause problems for their physical and emotional well-being. It is advised to provide an enclosure for a young or juvenile Leopard tortoise that measures at least 4 by 2 feet. But as it develops, the cage will need to be enlarged for the turtle. Due to their tendency to grow rather big, adult leopard tortoises should have an indoor cage that is at least 8 feet by 4 feet in order to provide them plenty of freedom for locomotion.

***Substrate:*** Enclosure ground covering, or substrate, is essential to permitting natural activities like burrowing and excavating. In order to give the right amount of humidity without being too wet, the substrate should be soft, easily plowed, and able to hold onto some moisture. Common selections for substrate used by Leopard tortoises include:

**- *Coconut Coir:*** Tortoises may safely chew through this natural fiber made from coconut husks, which retains moisture effectively.

- *Cypress Mulch:* This safe alternative adds a natural feel to the cage and aids with humidity maintenance.

- *Topsoil/Sand Mix:* A blend of organic topsoil and sand, free of chemicals or fertilizers, replicates the natural habitat of Leopard tortoises, facilitating their burrowing process.

Steer clear of substrates with oils that might hurt tortoises, such as cedar or pine shavings. To minimize respiratory problems, overly dry or dusty substrates should also be avoided.

*Heating and Lighting:* In order to maintain their body temperature and carry out vital processes like digestion, leopard tortoises need a warm environment. Since they are ectothermic, or cold-blooded, creatures, they must get their heat from outside sources. It is essential to provide enough lighting and warmth for interior enclosures.

- ***Basking Spot:*** Use a heat light to create a basking area that is kept between 95 and 100°F. The tortoise may now warm itself as required thanks to this. To allow the tortoise to go to colder regions as needed, place the heat lamp in one corner of the cage to create a temperature gradient.

- ***Ambient Temperature:*** During the day, the ambient temperature in the remaining enclosure should range from 75 to 85°F. Even while it may go as low as 70°F at night without harming the tortoises, try not to let them get too cold, particularly if they are younger.

***UVB illumination:*** Leopard tortoises need UVB illumination to create vitamin D3, which is required for calcium absorption and a healthy shell's growth. Without exposure to UVB sun, tortoises are susceptible to metabolic bone disease, a dangerous ailment that causes their shells to become fragile or malformed. A UVB lamp that covers at least 50% of the cage should be installed, and it should be left on for 10 to 12 hours per day.

***Humidity:*** Although native to desert areas, leopard tortoises nonetheless need some humidity, particularly in their younger years when they are more vulnerable to dehydration. A leopard tortoise's enclosure should have a humidity level of between 40% and 60%. By choosing a substrate that holds moisture and sprinkling the cage often, you can maintain humidity. Keep an eye out for excessive humidity levels as they might cause respiratory issues.

***Enrichment and Hide Areas:*** Provide your tortoise enrichment in the form of rocks, logs, and plants to promote natural behaviors and maintain mental stimulation. Leopard tortoises also need a safe haven in which to hide. Give them a hiding place or a cover so they can take a break from the heat.

### *Outside Covers*

In outdoor enclosures, leopard tortoises perform quite well, particularly in conditions that are comparable to their native environment. They may move around freely, eat on grass, and enjoy the natural sunshine that contains vital UVB rays when they are put up outside. Outside enclosures do, however, need additional precautions.

***Size and Fencing:*** For an adult tortoise, an outside enclosure has to be as big as possible, measuring at least 10 feet by 10 feet. Because leopard tortoises are powerful diggers, make sure the enclosure's walls are at least 12 inches below the surface to keep them from escaping. The minimum height of the walls to prevent the tortoise from climbing over them is 18 inches.

***Substrate:*** Grass and natural dirt provide excellent surfaces for outside enclosures. Since grass is what leopard tortoises feed on, make sure there is a variety of grass in the enclosure for them to consume. Additionally, you may grow plants that are safe for tortoises, such as clover and dandelion.

***Heating and cover:*** Although natural sunshine is beneficial for outdoor tortoises, they also need access to shade and cover to prevent overheating. Create shady spots using trees, shrubs, or man-made buildings. Give the tortoise access to a strong shelter as well so it may seek refuge from inclement weather, such as strong rain or freezing temperatures. During the winter months, you may need to bring your tortoise inside or offer extra warmth if the overnight lows in your location are very low.

*Water Source:* Make sure the outside enclosure always has a small water dish available. Because leopard tortoises like to drink and bathe in water, ensure the dish is both accessible and big enough to accommodate the tortoise properly. Change the water everyday to keep it clean.

*Predator Protection:* Dogs, raccoons, and other predatory birds of prey are among the predators that outdoor tortoises are susceptible to. Ascertain that the enclosure is safe from harm and secure. To keep predators out, you may need to construct more obstacles or cover the cage with wire mesh.

### Environmental Factors to Take Into Account

In both indoor and outdoor arrangements, it is crucial to keep a clean and safe environment for your Leopard tortoise. Eliminate food scraps and rubbish on a regular basis to stop the formation of germs and mold. Additionally, keep an eye on the enclosure's temperature, humidity, and illumination levels to make sure they stay within the ideal range. You can offer your Leopard tortoise the greatest chance for a long and healthy life by providing it with an appropriate home.

## *CHAPTER 6:*

# LEOPARD TORTOISES' HEALTH AND COMMON ILLNESSES

Although leopard tortoises are tough animals in general, they are prone to various health issues just like any other living thing. Maintaining the health of your tortoise depends on being aware of early warning indicators of disease and knowing how to avoid common ailments. This chapter will discuss the most typical health issues that leopard tortoises encounter, along with their symptoms and solutions for preserving general health.

### *Overall Health Surveillance*

Maintaining a regular check on your Leopard tortoise's health is essential to identifying any possible problems early on. A Leopard tortoise in good health will be energetic, vigilant, and voracious eaters. Its skin should be smooth, its shell solid, and its eyes clear. Abrupt changes in behavior, dietary patterns, or physical appearance may be a sign of a medical issue.

### *Indications of a Well-Being Leopard Tortoise:*
- Bright, clear eyes
- A flawless, rigid shell free of flaws
- Vigorous and attentive conduct - Abundant desire for grass and greenery - Consistent bowel motions
- Hydrated, smooth skin

Indices of Disease:

- Apathy or a reduction in activity

- An inability or unwillingness to eat

- A pliable or twisted shell

- Reduction of weight

- Wheezing, nasal discharge, or hard breathing

- Sunken look or swollen eyes

It's critical to get in touch with a reptile-focused veterinarian right away if you see any of these symptoms. Your tortoise's recovery may be significantly impacted by an early diagnosis and course of therapy.

### *Typical Health Problems*

Respiratory Infections: One of the most prevalent medical issues affecting Leopard tortoises is respiratory infection, especially in those housed in cages with low humidity or temperature. Symptoms of a respiratory infection include wheezing, nasal discharge, open-mouth breathing, and fatigue.

- *Causes:* High humidity and low temperatures are common causes of respiratory illnesses. The development of these illnesses may also be attributed to unclean cages and inadequate ventilation.

*Treatment:* See a veterinarian right away if your tortoise exhibits symptoms of a respiratory illness. They could recommend altering the enclosure configuration or prescribing antibiotics. Respiratory diseases may be avoided by keeping the enclosure clean and by regulating the humidity and temperature.

***Metabolic Bone Disease (MBD):*** When a tortoise's body does not get enough calcium or vitamin D3 to support normal bone and shell formation, it may result in metabolic bone disease, a dangerous ailment. Weak bones, soft or malformed shells, and in extreme instances, paralysis or death are the results of this disorder.

*- Causes:* A diet low in calcium or a lack of UVB sun exposure, which aids in the tortoise's synthesis of vitamin D3, are the causes of MBD. A deficiency of vitamin D3 prevents the tortoise from effectively absorbing calcium.

*- Treatment:* The best course of action for MBD is prevention. Give your tortoise a food strong in calcium, such as leafy greens, and make sure it gets access to UVB radiation.

Get in touch with your veterinarian right away for calcium supplements and therapy if your tortoise exhibits symptoms of MBD, such as a soft shell, abnormalities, or weakness.

***Shell Rot:*** An illness known as "shell rot" causes the tortoise's shell to deteriorate, becoming mushy and sometimes even breaking open. It is an illness caused by bacteria or fungi that may happen to tortoises housed in unclean, humid environments.

- ***Causes:*** A combination of poor hygiene and extended exposure to moisture, such as seen in a damp enclosure or water dish, may lead to shell rot. Moreover, abrasions or breaks in the shell may let germs or fungus in and lead to illness.

- ***Treatment:*** As directed by a veterinarian, treating shell rot entails washing the afflicted region and using antiseptics or antifungal lotions. In extreme situations, the veterinarian may have to extract dead tissue or provide medications. Keep the cage dry and clean, and check the shell for damage on a regular basis to prevent shell rot.

Like many other reptiles, leopard tortoises are susceptible to both internal and external parasites. Internal parasites like worms may cause weight loss, diarrhea, and lethargy by interfering with the digestive tract of the tortoise. Ticks and mites are examples of external parasites that may irritate skin and cause illnesses.

- *Causes:* Contaminated food, water, or substrate are common entry points for parasites.

Compared to captive-bred tortoises, wild-caught tortoises are more likely to contain parasites.

- ***Treatment:*** A veterinarian may identify internal parasites by routine fecal testing, and deworming medication can be administered. The veterinarian could suggest certain treatments, such mite sprays or baths, for exterior parasites. Parasites may be avoided by keeping the cage clean and sanitary, as well as by making sure the food and water are.

## Health Promotion

A balanced food, habitat maintenance, and routine health examinations are all important components of preventing health problems in Leopard tortoises. The following are essential actions to keep your tortoise healthy:

***Diet and Nutrition:*** Offer a diverse diet that consists of foods strong in calcium and fiber, such dark leafy greens, dandelion, and grasses. Fruits should not be fed since they are heavy in sugar and may upset your stomach. If there isn't enough calcium in your tortoise's diet, think about giving it supplements.

***UVB Lighting and Heating:*** Ensure your tortoise gets access to UVB lighting for 10-12 hours a day. This is necessary to stop MBD and absorb calcium. Additionally, to strengthen your tortoise's immune system, keep the habitat at the proper temperature for both basking and ambient conditions.

***Cleanliness and Hygiene:*** Regularly clean the enclosure to avoid the build-up of germs, mold, and parasites. Clean the water dish every day and replace the substrate as necessary. Steer clear of overwatering the substrate to stop shell rot from occurring.

***Frequent Vet Visits:*** It's a good idea to schedule routine vet visits, particularly for fecal testing and parasite screens, even if your tortoise seems healthy. Early identification of health concerns helps save later, more significant complications.

### Final Thoughts

Many of the frequent health issues that Leopard tortoises encounter may be avoided by giving them the right care and paying close attention to their health. Keeping your tortoise clean, feeding it a balanced food, and making sure the lighting and temperature are right can all help to keep it healthy. Do not wait to seek veterinarian treatment if you see any symptoms of sickness.

## CHAPTER 7:

# BEST PRACTICES AND TECHNIQUES FOR HANDLING LEOPARD TORTOISES

Although caring for leopard tortoises may seem simple, doing it incorrectly may lead to stress, harm, or even long-term behavioral changes in your pet. It is essential to comprehend the proper methods and guidelines for treating these creatures in a courteous and safe manner. This chapter will go over how to manage a Leopard tortoise properly, when to handle them, how to recognize stress signals in them, and what not to do while handling them. By the time you're done, you'll know how to communicate with your tortoise in a manner that fosters trust and reduces pain.

## *Reasons Why Care Must Be Taken When Handling*

Because they are solitary creatures by nature, leopard tortoises do not need or want human physical contact. Their natural responses to being touched often include retreating inside of themselves or acting erratically, both of which are indications of stress. Reptiles like tortoises do not have the same emotional attachment as pets like dogs or cats. Therefore, their requirements must be treated differently.

- *Physical Sensitivity:* Leopard tortoises are sensitive to being raised off the ground, even if their shells are strong. They are particularly susceptible when raised incorrectly, especially their tail, head, and legs.

- *Stress Response:* New or unexpected encounters quickly cause stress in tortoises, weakening their immune systems and increasing their susceptibility to disease.

### The Best Methods for Managing

Making sure the leopard tortoise feels safe and that you are not causing it undue distress is the first step in handling it correctly. The following are the suggested methods for picking up and handling your tortoise:

*1. Approach Calmly:* Always approach your tortoise from the front or side so it can see you before trying to raise it. Your tortoise may get stressed if it is startled by sudden movements.

*2. Use Two Hands:* When raising your Leopard tortoise, always use both hands. Put a strong hand under its shell close to its front legs and a loose one close to its rear legs. By doing this, the weight is distributed evenly and the tortoise doesn't have to struggle.

*3. Support the Entire Body:* Ensure that the tortoise has complete underbody support as you elevate it. Refrain from giving the tortoise an unpleasant or dangerous grasp on the sides. To make the tortoise feel safe, it is important to support the whole underside of the shell.

*4. keep it Near Your Body:* To prevent unintentional drops, keep the tortoise near your body once it has been raised. The tortoise may feel uneasy and struggle harder if you hold it far from your body.

*5. Minimize Time in the Air:* Make an effort to keep your turtle off the ground for as little time as possible. They may experience stress from prolonged handling, and if they don't feel supported, they could panic.

### Frequency of Handling

Since leopard tortoises are not gregarious by nature, treating them excessively might cause needless stress. Finding the right balance between restricting contact to what the tortoise can handle and handling it when required (for example, cleaning the cage or doing health checks) is crucial.

- *Frequency:* Handling your tortoise once or twice a week for short durations is typically adequate. Lower the frequency of handling if your turtle exhibits indications of discomfort, including hiding for prolonged periods of time or becoming less active.

- *Handling for Health:* Regular handling is required for health examinations, particularly to keep an eye out for any anomalies, damage, or infections in the shell.

## *Indices of Stress Related to Managing*

Preventing injury to Leopard tortoises requires an understanding of their stress indicators. Any of the following actions, either during or after handling, may indicate that your turtle is overwhelmed:

- ***Hissing or Heavy Breathing:*** When a tortoise perceives stress or danger, it may hiss.

- ***Withdrawing into the Shell:*** Although this is a normal protective response, it shows discomfort or worry when it happens often.

- ***Flailing Limbs:*** Your tortoise may feel uneasy or frightened if it rapidly kicks or waves its legs while being handled.

- ***Lethargy Post-Handling:*** If your tortoise hides or remains motionless for an extended period of time after being handled, it may be under stress.

**Precautions to Take When Managing**

There are several things you should never do while working with your Leopard tortoise in order to keep them happy and healthy:

*1. Never Lift by the Shell Only:* It hurts and is unpleasant for the tortoise to be lifted by gripping its shell from the top. It may injure it and put pressure on its spine and legs.

*2. Avoid Sudden Movements:* When being handled, tortoises particularly detest abrupt or jerky movements. While working with them, always take your time and be calm.

*3. Do Not Drop:* A Leopard tortoise's shell, limbs, or internal organs may sustain serious damage if it is dropped, even from a little height. Just in case, always handle your tortoise near the ground or on a soft surface.

**4. *Limited touching During Illness:*** If your tortoise is exhibiting symptoms of disease, try to avoid touching it too much unless it's essential for getting it to the veterinarian. Taking care of a sick or stressed tortoise might make it worse.

## Advantages of Correct Handling

Handling your Leopard tortoise may be advantageous if done properly. It enables you to keep a careful eye on the physical health of your tortoise, look for any wounds or anomalies, and clean its shell as required. Your tortoise may get used to human contact over time, which will facilitate regular health examinations and cage upkeep.

- ***Bonding:*** Although leopard tortoises and people don't connect in the same ways as other pets, a degree of trust may be developed via calm and considerate handling. With time, your tortoise could become less afraid and more tolerant of handling.

- ***Health Monitoring:*** By touching your tortoise often, you can keep an eye out for any symptoms of disease or damage that could be missed with routine care.

### *Final Thoughts*

Patience, attention, and consideration for the animal's limits are necessary while caring for your leopard tortoise. You can make sure that your tortoise stays comfortable and healthy by using the right methods, minimizing the frequency of handling, and being alert to symptoms of stress. Always remember that your tortoise's welfare comes first, so treat them with kindness and consideration.

# *CHAPTER 8:*

# EXPECTATIONS FOR BREEDING LEOPARD TORTOISES

It takes a thorough grasp of leopard tortoises' biology, reproductive behavior, and the particular environmental conditions they need to successfully mate and produce eggs to undertake the delicate and intricate task of breeding them. This chapter will walk you through what to anticipate during the mating season, from courting behaviors to egg incubation and hatchling care, whether you are an experienced breeder or a hobbyist.

### *Recognizing the Reproduction of Leopard Tortoises*

Due to their sexual dimorphism, male and female leopard tortoises may be identified by morphological traits. In order to help in mounting during mating, males often develop longer tails and a concave plastron (the underside of the shell). Generally speaking, females are bigger and have shorter tails.

*- Sexual Maturity:* Leopard tortoises mature sexually between the ages of 10 and 15. Males become reproductively active at roughly 12 inches in length, whereas females attain reproductive maturity closer to 14 inches. Therefore, size is a more accurate predictor of maturity than age.

*- Breeding Season:* The rainy season encourages mating activities, which is when leopard tortoises normally breed in their native environment. Breeders may mimic this in captivity by modifying the enclosure's humidity and temperature settings.

## *Mating and Courtship Behavior*

Leopard tortoises have harsh courtships, especially when it comes from the male's perspective. In an attempt to establish dominance, the male will pursue the female and may bite her legs or shell. He may also produce loud grunting sounds. When she's ready to mate, the female will cease trying to run away from the male and let him mount her.

***Courting Rituals:*** Although the male leopard tortoise's courting actions may seem hostile, they are an inherent aspect of the tortoise's reproductive cycle. Although biting and nudging are frequent, caution should be used to make sure the female is not unduly agitated or hurt.

*- **Mating Process:*** When the female is ready, the male mounts her and uses his concave plastron to balance on her shell. The male emits loud vocalizations throughout the several-minute-long mating ritual. It is not unusual for many days to pass between mating attempts.

## Setting Up the Nesting Location

The female will start looking for an appropriate nesting location after a successful mating. After mating, the female will usually become restless and pace the cage while excavating test nests for 30 to 60 days before nesting.

**- *Nesting Area Requirements:*** The female must be able to dig a deep hole to deposit her eggs, and the nesting site must contain loose, sandy soil. She could hold onto her eggs if the substrate in her habitat is too shallow or hard, which might result in health issues such as egg binding (dystocia).

**- *Nesting Box:*** To replicate the natural habitat in captivity, you may give a nesting box filled with a combination of sand and dirt. The female should be able to move around and dig comfortably in the box.

***Incubation and Laying of Eggs***

Depending on their size and condition, female leopard tortoises may lay anywhere from five to thirty eggs in a clutch. The female will meticulously cover the nest with dirt once the eggs are placed, then resume her regular activity. Leopard tortoises do not remain to defend the nest, in contrast to some other species.

*Egg Collection:* To maintain ideal humidity and temperature control, breeders often gather the eggs from the captive animals and store them in an incubator. It's important to handle the eggs with caution because spinning them might disturb the growing embryo within.

*Incubation Conditions:* For optimal development, leopard tortoise eggs need to be incubated at a temperature between 82 and 86°F (28 and 30°C) with high humidity levels. The length of the incubation period varies from 90 to 120 days according on temperature.

## *Care for Hatchlings*

The newborn tortoises, known as hatchlings, are quite fragile after the eggs hatch. A yolk sac that is connected to the plastron of hatchlings at birth supplies them with food throughout their early days of existence. This is the moment to leave them alone.

- *Hatchling Housing:* Hatchlings need a separate cage that has the right humidity, lighting, and warmth. To protect their fragile shells, the cage has to feature a shallow water dish, hiding places, and a soft substrate.

*- food:* To promote their quick growth and shell formation, hatchlings need a food high in calcium. For their dietary requirements, a blend of commercially available tortoise food, grasses, and dark leafy greens is optimal.

### The Difficulties of Raising Leopard Tortoises

Raising Leopard tortoises has some difficulties. Egg binding, inappropriate incubation conditions, and hatchlings that do not flourish are typical issues. Additionally, producing Leopard tortoises requires a significant time commitment due to their lengthy incubation period and sluggish development rate.

*- Egg Binding:* A female may hold onto her eggs if she cannot locate a suitable nesting place. This might result in major health problems. This

may be avoided with regular veterinarian examinations and by making sure the nesting area is suitable.

*Incubation Failures:* Eggs may not hatch or may give birth to malformed hatchlings if they are not incubated at the proper temperature or humidity conditions. Throughout the incubation stage, it is important to keep a constant eye on the incubator.

-   *Hatchling Mortality:* Malnutrition, dehydration, and shell abnormalities are the main causes of death for young tortoises. For them to survive, the first few months of life must be spent receiving the best care possible.

*Final Thoughts*

The experience of breeding leopard tortoises may be quite fulfilling, but it does need meticulous preparation, perseverance, and commitment. There are several things to take into account, ranging from comprehending courting and mating behaviors to setting up the ideal environment for egg incubation and hatchling care. Breeding Leopard tortoises provides the chance to support the survival of this amazing species and experience the magic of seeing new life emerge for those who are prepared to put in the necessary time and effort.

## *CHAPTER 9:*

# LEOPARD TORTOISE NUTRITION AND FEEDING

### *Overview of the Leopard Tortoise Food*

A balanced diet is essential for the development, well-being, and lifespan of leopard tortoises. In contrast to some other domesticated animals, tortoises have nutritional needs that are based on their natural environments, which are mostly composed of herbaceous plants. It is essential for every owner of a leopard tortoise to comprehend the dietary requirements of their pet and how to feed them a diverse and adequate food.

### Natural Diet

Native to Africa's savannas and grasslands, leopard tortoises (Stigmochelys pardalis) feed on a wide range of grasses, herbs, and leafy greens. Their natural diet is low in protein and abundant in fiber, which promotes good digestion and guards against obesity. In the wild, they also ingest flowers, fruits, and succulent plants, particularly during the rainy season when such items are more available.

### Crucial Elements of Nutrition

*1. Fiber:* An essential part of a Leopard tortoise's diet, fiber promotes healthy digestion and guards against gastrointestinal problems. The majority of their diets should consist of high-fiber items like hay and grasses. Berries, orchard grass, and Timothy hay are great options that closely resemble their natural eating habits.

**2. *Vitamins and Calcium:*** Both bone health and metabolic processes depend on calcium. Metabolic bone disease is a condition marked by weak and malformed bones that may result from a calcium deficit. A calcium-to-phosphorus ratio of around 2:1 is necessary for tortoises. Calcium-rich leafy greens include kale, collard greens, and dandelion greens. Furthermore, giving your tortoise a calcium supplement— especially one that has vitamin D3—will help ensure that it gets enough.

**3. *Low Protein:*** Leopard tortoises don't need a diet heavy in protein, in contrast to several other reptiles. Shell abnormalities and renal issues might result from eating too much protein. It's important to choose commercial tortoise pellets carefully so that the protein content is low—usually less than 12%.

**4. *Hydration:*** Freshwater should always be accessible, even though tortoises get some moisture from their diet. It is important to offer a small water dish for the tortoise to sip from and soak in so that it may stay well hydrated.

### *Suggested Foods*

In order to make sure your Leopard tortoise gets all the nutrition it needs, you must provide a diversified diet. Here are some foods that are suggested:

*1. Leafy greens: -* Collard greens: rich in vitamins and minerals.

Dandelion Greens: High in fiber and calcium.

*- Mustard Greens:* A wholesome green choice.

**Kale:** Rich in vitamins, however because of its increased oxalate level, it should only be served seldom.

*2. Grasses and Hays:* Timothy Hay: A mainstay of the fiber world.

*- Hay from Bermuda Grass:* An additional excellent fiber source.

*3. Weeds and Flowers: - Hibiscus Flowers:* Nutritious and safe.

*- Dandelion Flowers:* Turtles love these edible flowers.

*- Nasturtiums:* Tasty and colorful for turtles.

*4. Fruits (in moderation): - Melons: A cool delight.*

*- Berries:* Due to their high sugar content, they should only be used in moderation to provide vitamins.

*5. Commercial Tortoise Food: -* Search for low-protein, high-fiber choices. Always look for artificial additions in the ingredient list.

*Getting the Diet Ready*

When making your Leopard tortoise's diet, there are various criteria to follow to ensure their food is safe and nutritious:

*- Wash All Greens:* To get rid of pollutants or pesticides, give all veggies and greens a thorough wash.

*- Cut Food Correctly:* Cut food into manageable bits for easy intake, particularly for younger tortoises.

*- Rotate Foods:* To keep things interesting and avoid monotony, rotate meal products on a regular basis.

## Timetable for Feeding

Leopard tortoises need a regular feeding plan to survive. Adult tortoises may be fed every other day, while young tortoises should be fed every day. A variety of leafy greens, grasses, and sometimes fruits or flowers may be offered during a feeding session. In order to keep the cage clean and avoid food spoiling, it is important to remove any uneaten food immediately.

## *Supplements and Extra Nutritious Requirements*

Supplements could be needed in addition to a diversified diet to make sure your tortoise gets all the nutrition it needs:

*Calcium Supplements:* A calcium supplement needs to be sprinkled over their meals many times a week, ideally together with vitamin D3.
- *Multivitamins:* To make up for any nutritional shortfalls, provide a reptile multivitamin once a week.

### *Monitoring Eating Routines*

Keep a tight eye on your tortoise's dietary habits. A healthy tortoise will be energetic and ready to eat. Your tortoise may have underlying health problems that need to be attended to by a veterinarian if it gets listless, refuses to eat, or exhibits symptoms of weight loss.

## *Final Thoughts*

Your Leopard tortoise's health and wellbeing depend on eating a food that is well-balanced. You may contribute to your tortoise's long and healthy life by giving it a choice of high-fiber, low-protein diets and the right supplements. The secret to providing excellent care for tortoises in captivity is to comprehend their natural diet and modify it to suit their demands.

## *CHAPTER 10:*

# LEOPARD TORTOISES' HEALTH AND COMMON DISEASES

### *Recognizing the Health of Leopard Tortoises*

For the lifespan and general well-being of your Leopard tortoise, you must keep it healthy. Any owner of a tortoise must be knowledgeable about frequent illnesses and health concerns and observe their pet on a regular basis. An overview of common health issues and precautions to keep your tortoise healthy is given in this chapter.

## Indices of a Tamarind Turtle's Well-Being

Knowing the telltale symptoms of a healthy Leopard tortoise is crucial before delving into health-related topics.

**1. Active Behavior:** In general, healthy tortoises exhibit normal behavior and are rather active, investigating their surroundings.

**2. Healthy Shell:** There should be no fractures, lesions, or undue softness on the smooth, clean shell.

**3. Clear Eyes and Nose:** Eyes should be clear and bright, while the nostrils should be free of discharge.

*4. Regular Eating:* A robust appetite is a reliable sign of well-being.

*5. Correct Hydration:* A healthy, well-hydrated tortoise should have a wet look.

### Typical Health Problems

*1. Respiratory Infections:* One of the most prevalent medical conditions affecting tortoises is respiratory infection. Lethargy, open-mouth breathing, wheezing, and nasal discharge are among the symptoms. The enclosure's drafts, humidity, or temperature may all contribute to these diseases.

*Prevention:* Keep the enclosure's temperature and humidity at suitable levels. Aim for enough ventilation while keeping drafts at bay. For treatment options, speak with a veterinarian if symptoms arise.

**2. *Metabolic Bone Disease (MBD):*** Deficits in calcium and vitamin D3 create MBD, a dangerous illness that results in malformed shells and weakening of the bones. Soft shells, limb swelling, and trouble moving are among the symptoms.

***Prevention:*** Make sure you have access to UVB sunshine for the production of vitamin D3, and feed a calcium-rich, well-balanced diet. Supplementing on a regular basis could also be required.

**3. *Shell Rot:*** A fungal or bacterial infection that damages the tortoise's shell is known as shell rot. Discoloration, an unpleasant smell, and soft spots on the shell are among the symptoms. Shell rot may result in serious diseases if treatment is not received.

*Prevention:* Keep the cage dry and tidy, and don't let the tortoise rest on damp materials. For treatment, see a veterinarian if shell rot is suspected.

*4. Worms and Parasites:* Both internal and external parasites may have an adverse effect on tortoises, resulting in anorexia, lassitude, and decreased appetite. Unusual behavior or obvious worms in the feces are possible indicators.

*Prevention:* Regular veterinarian check-ups and fecal examinations may help monitor for parasites. Keep the surroundings clean and refrain from overfeeding to lower the possibility of internal parasites.

**5. *Obesity:*** Overfeeding, especially on diets high in protein, may result in obesity in tortoises, which can cause health problems including deformed shells and decreased mobility.

***Prevention:*** Watch feeding quantities and provide a diet rich in fiber and low in protein. Encourage regular exercise by offering a large and interesting atmosphere.

**6. *Dehydration:*** Conditions such as low water intake or dry air may lead to dehydration. Lethargy, sunken eyes, and dry skin are among the symptoms.

*Prevention:* Consistently provide fresh water and keep an eye on the enclosure's humidity levels. Another way to keep the tortoise hydrated is to regularly submerge it in shallow, lukewarm water.

### Frequent Medical Exams

You must take your Leopard tortoise to the vet on a regular basis to ensure its health. A veterinarian with expertise in reptiles may provide insightful guidance on nutrition, habitat maintenance, and prophylactic treatment. At examinations, the veterinarian is able to:

*Physical Exams:* A comprehensive check of the tortoise's limbs, body, and shell.

- *Fecal Exams:* To look for gastrointestinal problems or parasites.

*- **Blood Tests:*** To keep track of nutritional status and general health.

## *Signs That Require Immediate Veterinary Attention*

For the sake of your tortoise's health, you must know when to seek veterinary attention. See a veterinarian right once if you see any of the following symptoms:

- Extended lethargy or idleness
- Severe breathing symptoms, such as open-mouth breathing and wheezing
- Abrupt fluctuations in weight or appetite
- Atypical shell state (discoloration, soft patches)
- Inexplicable injuries or bleeding

## *Preventative Actions*

*1.Appropriate Habitat:* Establish a setting that supports a healthy lifestyle by providing the right humidity, lighting, and temperature. To help with the production of vitamin D3, make use of UVB lighting.

*2. Balanced Diet:* To avoid nutritional deficits and health problems, provide a diversified, balanced diet.

*3. Regular Monitoring:* Keep an eye out for any behavioral or physical changes in your tortoise. Maintaining a log of your tortoise's weight, feeding patterns, and any changes may aid in the early detection of health problems.

*4. Hygiene :* Keep your living space tidy by routinely getting rid of trash and uneaten meals.

To stop germs from growing, clean the water dish every day.

**5. *Socialization and Enrichment:*** Your tortoise's general wellbeing may be improved by offering socialization and mental stimulation via interaction and enrichment.

### *Final Thoughts*

Your Leopard tortoise's long-term enjoyment and vigor greatly depend on its health. You can guarantee your tortoise has a happy and healthy life by being aware of common health conditions, identifying symptoms of sickness, and taking preventative action. Healthy food, a clean living space, and routine veterinary care are necessary for successful Leopard tortoise keeping.

## *CHAPTER 11:*

# LEOPARD TORTOISE BREEDING

### *An Overview of Breeding Leopard Tortoises*

For devoted tortoise owners, breeding Leopard tortoises (Stigmochelys pardalis) may be a fulfilling task. It does, however, need a deep knowledge of their reproductive habits, appropriate handling during mating, and the requirements of hatchlings. The subtleties of breeding leopard tortoises will be covered in detail in this chapter, along with preparation for breeding, mating habits, egg-laying, incubation, and hatchling care.

### *Getting Ready for Breeding*

Leopard tortoise owners need to make sure they are ready before trying to mate their creatures. Take into account the following elements:

*1. Age and Maturity:* Although this may vary, turtles normally achieve sexual maturity between the ages of 5 and 7. It's possible for men to develop a little bit before women. Before trying to mate, it is essential to wait until both tortoises are completely developed, since juvenile tortoises may not have the physical capacity to reproduce or care for babies.

*2. Health Check:* To make sure the male and female tortoises are healthy and free of parasites or illnesses, they should get a full veterinarian inspection before mating. There is a greater chance of successful reproduction and healthy progeny raising in healthy tortoises.

**3.Appropriate environment:** A suitable environment that can comfortably fit both tortoises is necessary for breeding. This area should be more roomy than their typical enclosure, with plenty of material for digging, hiding places, and basking spaces.

**4. Dietary Considerations:** Breeding tortoises need proper nourishment. A diet heavy in fiber, low in protein, and high in vitamins and calcium will keep the tortoises healthy and prepared for reproduction. Taking calcium and vitamin supplements might be very helpful at this time.

**Mating Patterns**

When the tortoises are mature and healthy, watch how they mate:

*1. Courting Rituals:* Males often engage in courting activities throughout the breeding season, such as head bobbing, prodding, and trying to mount the female. The male and female tortoises must form a relationship during this courting.

*2. Mating Process:* The male will crawl atop the female's shell and position himself correctly for mating when she is receptive. It may take many days for there to be several copulations throughout this lengthy procedure. Due to the intensity of this behavior, owners should keep a careful eye on it.

### The Laying of Eggs

Eventually, the female turtle will deposit eggs after a successful mating episode. When laying eggs, there are a number of crucial factors to take into account:

**1. Nest Preparation:** Females naturally search for a good spot to deposit their eggs, typically excavating a nest in the substrate. Give the female a place to dig and feel safe to make her nest, preferably with loose dirt or substrate. To encourage the female to deposit her eggs, the nesting place should be distant from any disruptions.

**2. Egg Laying:** Although this amount may fluctuate, leopard tortoises often lay three to twelve eggs every clutch. Once deposited, the eggs should not be moved since they are leathery. The female may depart the nesting place after depositing her eggs and covering them with substrate.

**3. Observation:** It's crucial to keep an eye out for any indications of suffering in the female after she lays her eggs. After laying, some females may have problems, so owners should be ready to provide medical treatment if needed.

**Egg Incubation**

After the eggs are deposited, their incubation becomes the main focus:

**1. Collecting Eggs:** You may gently excavate the eggs and deposit them in an incubator if the nesting location is not perfect or if you want to boost the odds of a successful hatch. To prevent harming the developing embryos, always handle the eggs carefully and maintain them orientated in the same direction as when they were deposited.

*2. Incubation Conditions:* The best incubation temperature for Leopard tortoise eggs is between 85°F to 88°F (29°C to 31°C). Humidity levels in incubators should be consistently maintained between 70% and 80%. Eggs may dry out if the humidity is too low, while mold may form if the humidity is too high.

*3. Incubation Duration:* Depending on the surroundings, the incubation time for Leopard tortoise eggs usually lasts between 60 and 90 days. To guarantee a good hatch, it is essential to keep an eye on the eggs throughout this time.

*Taking Care of Egg Laylings*

After the eggs hatch, the hatchlings' survival depends critically on their care:

*1. Hatchling Habitat:* Make sure the hatchlings have a safe, secure, and suitable-sized enclosure that is kept apart from other enclosures. A shallow water dish, hiding places, and suitable lighting and warmth should all be part of this environment. In general, hatchlings need temperatures between 85°F and 90°F (29°C and 32°C), which are warmer than those of adults.

*2. Feeding Hatchlings:* Hatchlings should be given a diet that is smaller and easier to handle than that of adult tortoises. Present a variety of finely chopped vegetables, leafy greens, and grasses. To promote healthy development, always have fresh water available, and think about sprinkling meals with calcium powder.

**3. *Monitoring development* :** Pay special attention to the health and development of the hatchlings. Frequent weight checks and activity level monitoring will aid in the early detection of any possible health problems. As soon as a hatchling shows symptoms of disease or is not thriving, take it to the veterinarian.

**Final Thoughts**

Raising Leopard tortoises may be a rewarding and instructive endeavor. Owners of tortoises may effectively breed these intriguing animals and guarantee the well-being of their young with the correct information, planning, and care. The overall success of the breeding process will be aided by proper attention to mating behaviors, egg-laying, incubation, and hatchling care, enabling owners to take pleasure in the experiences of parenting Leopard tortoises.

## CHAPTER 12:

# THE PLEASURES AND DIFFICULTIES OF OWNING A LEOPARD TORTOISE

### Overview of Owning a Tortoise

Having a Leopard tortoise (Stigmochelys pardalis) as a pet may be quite fulfilling. In addition to being entertaining to see, these animals need their caretakers to provide them constant attention and dedication. The pleasures and obligations of owning a leopard tortoise are discussed in this chapter, with special attention paid to the need for appropriate care, the psychological benefits of companionship, and the moral ramifications of owning tortoises as pets.

### The Pleasures of Keeping a Leopard Tortoise as a Pet

**1.  *distinctive Personalities:*** Each leopard tortoise is distinctive due to their own personalities. Observing their tortoise's habits, eccentricities, and interactions with their surroundings may provide great pleasure to its owners. From their slow, methodical motions to their keen inquiry, tortoises may become intriguing companions.

**2. *Long lifetime:*** The remarkable lifetime of Leopard tortoises is one of the best things about having one of these animals. These tortoises become enduring companions for generations when given the right care, since they may live over 50 years. Deep ties may develop between the owner and the tortoise because of its longevity.

**3. *Educational Possibilities:*** Having a Leopard tortoise may be a great way to learn, especially for families with young children. Learning about the nutritional demands, environmental requirements, and behavioral patterns of tortoises promotes responsible pet management and cultivates a respect for nature.

**4. *minimal Maintenance:*** Leopard tortoises are comparatively minimal maintenance pets as compared to many conventional pets. Compared to dogs or cats, they often need less daily care after their habitat is built and their food demands are satisfied. They are thus appropriate for those who lead hectic lives yet nonetheless want a pet.

**5. *Connection to Nature:*** Having a tortoise in the home provides a special connection with the natural world. Owners may learn about the value of conservation and the function that tortoises perform in their ecosystems by seeing their animals in their native habitats.

### *Ownership of Tortoises' Responsibilities*

Although having a Leopard tortoise is a joyful endeavor, prospective owners must be aware of the following important obligations:

**1. *Long-Term Commitment:*** Owning a Leopard tortoise requires a long-term commitment due to its lifetime of 50 years or more. Potential owners should think about whether they can provide the necessary care for a tortoise over such a long time, as well as any possible changes to their living arrangements or personal circumstances.

**2. *Correct environment Maintenance:*** Your tortoise's health and wellbeing depend on you providing a suitable environment. This entails maintaining ideal humidity, temperature, and illumination levels. To avoid health problems, the habitat must be regularly cleaned and observed.

**3. *Dietary Needs:*** One of the main responsibilities of owning a tortoise is to make sure it is fed a healthy, balanced diet. To avoid nutritional deficits and other health issues, owners need to do their homework on suitable food products and keep an eye on their tortoise's diet.

**4. *veterinarian Care:*** It's important to keep an eye on your tortoise's health with routine veterinarian examinations. To get the essential medical attention and guidance, owners should choose a veterinarian with expertise with reptiles.

**5. *Legal and Ethical Considerations:*** The Convention on International Trade in Endangered Species (CITES) provides protection for leopard tortoises. Owners must therefore make sure that the tortoises they purchase are lawfully obtained from trustworthy breeders or rescues. It is essential to educate oneself on the moral implications of owning tortoises, particularly the value of conservation.

**6. *Socialization and involvement:*** Although they are not as rigorous as dogs or cats, leopard tortoises nonetheless gain from mild owner involvement. This might include providing for their care, feeding them, and letting them experience the world outside of their cage in a secure setting. Owners need to acquaint themselves with their tortoise-like handling tolerance to prevent tension.

**7. *Identifying Health Concerns:*** It's essential that you keep a close eye on your tortoise's health. By being aware of the symptoms of sickness, owners may seek veterinarian treatment as soon as possible. These symptoms include changes in appetite, lethargy, and abnormal shell conditions. Early identification of health disorders requires regular monitoring of behavior and physical appearance.

**Creating a Connection with Your Turtle**

Forming a relationship with your Leopard tortoise may improve your ownership experience in general. The following advice can help to strengthen that bond:

*1. Routine Interaction:* Create a schedule that involves communicating with your tortoise on a regular basis. Trust may be developed by allowing them to spend time in their cage, providing food, and gently touching them when they feel comfortable.

*2. Observation :* Spend some time watching your turtle in its natural environment. Observing them investigate, enjoy, and engage with their surroundings may help you get a deeper understanding of their actions and character traits.

**3. *Outdoor Exploration:*** Let your tortoise explore outdoors in a safe location if it's acceptable and safe to do so. Spending time outside under supervision may improve their general quality of life and stimulate their minds.

**4. *Patience:*** It takes time and patience to form a friendship with a tortoise. You may build a strong bond with your pet by being aware of their needs and respecting their limits.

### *Final Thoughts*

Taking care of a Leopard tortoise involves duty, fun, and education. They are exceptional companions because of their distinct personalities, lengthy lifespans, and relationships to the natural world. However, potential owners must be aware of the obligations that come with turtle ownership, including long-term care, habitat preservation, and ethical issues. People may make a happy and satisfying life for themselves and their cherished tortoises by accepting the perks and obligations of owning Leopard tortoises.

## *CHAPTER 13*

# FREQUENTLY ASKED QUESTION AND ANSWERS (FAQS)

This is a collection of 12 often asked questions (FAQs) concerning caring for leopard tortoises, especially those that pertain to Chapter 13, along with thorough responses.

*Commonly Asked Questions (FAQs) on the Care of Leopard Tortoises*

*1. What are the fundamental needs for a Leopard tortoise's home?*

*Reaction:*

A large, safe cage that closely resembles the leopard tortoise's native environment is necessary for housing one. Digging is a natural action, thus the cage should contain a substantial base, such as dirt or grass. It should also include a colder section where the tortoise may control its body temperature and a basking area with a heat lamp to keep the temperature between 85°F and 90°F (29°C and 32°C). Always have access to fresh water and places to hide out that are constructed out of logs or rocks. Enclosures outside are quite useful as long as they are safe from predators and secure.

***2. What kind of food and how frequently should I feed my Leopard tortoise?***

***Reaction:***

Feeding should be done every day for leopard tortoises, especially in their early developing years. High-fiber grasses, leafy greens (such collard greens, dandelion greens, and endive), and a limited quantity of vegetables make up the majority of a suitable diet. Fruits and foods rich in protein should be avoided since they may cause health problems. In order to maintain healthy shell development and avoid metabolic bone disease, owners can think about dusting their food with calcium supplements and making sure that fresh, clean water is always accessible.

### 3. What symptoms point to a sick Leopard tortoise?

### Reaction:

Leopard tortoises may exhibit a variety of symptoms when they are unwell, but frequent ones include changes in the look of their shell (softness, discolouration, or strange growths), lack of appetite, lethargy, abnormal feces, and respiratory problems (such as wheezing or nasal discharge). For an accurate diagnosis and course of treatment, it is imperative that you speak with a veterinarian who has expertise with reptiles if you see any of these symptoms.

### 4. Are leopard tortoises compatible with other tortoises or reptiles in the home?

### Reaction:

Although it is possible to keep leopard tortoises in homes with other kinds of tortoises, it is crucial to make sure that the sizes, temperaments, and environmental requirements of each animal are suitable. Combining different species may cause tension, resource rivalry, and even the spread of disease. It is normally advised to keep Leopard tortoises separately for best health and wellbeing.

## 5. What sort of illumination are necessary for Leopard tortoises?

### Reaction:

For optimal health, leopard tortoises need both artificial UVB lighting and natural sunshine. A UVB light must be provided for around 10 to 12 hours per day if the animal is housed inside in order to promote calcium metabolism and vitamin D production. Tortoises run the danger of acquiring metabolic bone disease if they don't receive enough UVB rays. Allowing them to spend time outside in the sun (as long as they are watched after and shielded from predators) may be very beneficial to their health.

### 6. How can I determine a Leopard tortoise's age?

### Reaction:

Leopard tortoises lack obvious outward indicators, making it difficult to pinpoint their precise age. On the other hand, counting the growth rings on their scutes—the bony plates on their shells—is a popular technique. Though diet and environment may have an impact on this strategy, each ring typically represents a year of development. The shells of juvenile tortoises are typically smoother, but the growth patterns of adult tortoises are more prominent.

### 7. What temperature range is best for the cage of a Leopard tortoise?

*Reaction:*

Leopard tortoises like a temperature gradient that consists of a warmer section that stays between 70°F and 75°F (21°C and 24°C) and a basking area that is kept between 85°F and 90°F (29°C and 32°C). For tortoises to properly control their body temperature, which is essential for their metabolic functions, they must maintain this temperature range. Although it may become a little colder at night, the temperature shouldn't go below 65°F (18°C).

**8. How long will a Leopard tortoise live to be, and what can I do to make sure they do?**

*Reaction:*

With the right care, leopard tortoises may live for more than 50 years. Owners should provide their pets with a large, safe environment, balanced food, frequent veterinarian checkups, and enough UVB lighting to guarantee a long, healthy life. The general well-being of the tortoises will also be enhanced by maintaining a clean environment and keeping an eye out for any symptoms of disease.

**9. Are creatures like leopard tortoises social? Can they be kept with others?**

**Reaction:**

Animals like dogs or cats are sociable creatures, but not leopard tortoises. They do not create social relationships, although they may live in harmony with other tortoises. Make sure there is enough room if they are kept together to avoid tension and competitiveness. To provide them the greatest care and lower the possibility of violence or territory issues, it is often preferable to keep them alone.

## 10. How should my Leopard tortoise be ready for winter?

### Reaction:

Leopard tortoises naturally hibernate, and in preparation, they progressively reduce their food intake as the temperature decreases. Ensure they are healthy and free from parasites before hibernation time. Make sure they have a secure spot to burrow and provide them with a constant temperature-controlled habitat, preferably between 50°F and 60°F (10°C to 15°C). While they are hibernating, keep an eye on them and see a veterinarian if you have any concerns.

### 11. How do I handle refusing to eat a Leopard tortoise?

### Reaction:

A leopard tortoise that refuses to eat may be a sign of stress, disease, or an inappropriate habitat. Examine the habitat's parameters first, such as its temperature, humidity, and kind of food. Make sure there are no indications of sickness or stress. See a veterinarian for additional assessment and advice if the tortoise refuses food for more than a few days.

### 12. How can I make sure the food my Leopard tortoise is fed is balanced?

### Reaction:

Make sure your Leopard tortoise eats a healthy diet by emphasizing leafy greens and other high-fiber grasses. Fruits and foods rich in protein should be avoided since they may cause health problems. Add a variety of greens, such as collard greens, kale, and dandelion leaves. Ensure that you offer access to fresh water and consider periodic calcium supplements to maintain healthy shell development. Keep an eye on their health and modify their food as necessary.

www.ingramcontent.com/pod-product-compliance
Lightning Source LLC
Chambersburg PA
CBHW061351250726

48657CB00004B/1429